Dreaming of North Beach
(from Corporate America)

Dreaming of
North Beach
(from Corporate America)

Deno Gell

First published in 2025 by
Gell Studio Presents™

ISBN (paperback): 979-8-9987997-0-9
ISBN (ebook): 979-8-9987997-1-6

Book designed and typeset by InsideStudio26.com

Dedicated to all of those staring at the clock waiting for lunch…

Contents

A Friend in the Night

The cable car lines clattered and
hummed along to their own rhythm.

It was 3 a.m. and I just left Hawaii West,
angry again that the bill was so high.

How the hell did that happen?
I thought everyone was my friend tonight.

This was the best time to see
North Beach and Chinatown.

City lights bright,
tracks buzzing.
Nobody, not a soul around.

Bay Bridge lights flicker in the distance
like a warning sign for the road ahead.

I always imagined the humming
of the tracks at 3 a.m.
as a great way to close out an album.
The perfect outro.
It had to be 3 a.m.
or it wouldn't sound right.

I stumbled up to Powell and Washington St.
Prime corner for track humming.

I was lucky: at that moment
down the hill came a test car.
No tourists at that hour, just the car
and the conductor.

It trudged downhill at me
from Washington
and I gave him the salute,
then the point,
and he knew what to do.

He pulled the brake lever,
saluted me back,
and then he rang that goddamn bell
with the conviction of a man
who'd just forgotten
all the wrong he'd ever done—
as the cable car
picked up speed
and hit the turn onto Powell,
bound for Clay.

That's the only free nightcap in San Francisco
and nobody,
nobody can ever take that away from me.

Corporate America, Baby!

Salesforce, email, Zoom, and Slack
I'm just another company hack

Paycheck, bootlickers, goals all day
I'm somewhere else, but the songs don't pay

401(k), meetings, commute, and lunch
It's a "unicorn," they say—just don't drink the punch

Another goodbye, to another good friend,
Funds cut, lights out, and it's breadline again

Low Serotonin

Tanner was butchering basic guitar chords
on the sofa.

Brock was hanging from the pull-up bar
above the conference room door.

I was pretending to work,
pelted with Nerf gun darts by Taylor—
who was, I guess,

doing what people did at startups.

Meanwhile, Blake and Todd
were locked into a ping-pong battle
while the Michelin-starred leftovers
sat nearby—

wasted and on their way out the door,
just how I wished to be.

The middle managers,
over craft brews,
were huddled in a conference
room across the hall discussing

pipeline metrics and
sales strategy

with dreams of an IPO on the horizon.

Madison, the only competent
Account Executive on the team,
smashed the stupid gong
in the center of the open office and yelled,
"I closed another deal!"

We needed more Madisons
but hired too many Todds
and the company's funding
ran out nine months later.

Tanner played on.

American Ingenuity

I stood there angry—
face and body getting hammered
by the cold, relentless wind.

If I didn't know I was standing on
the Golden Gate Bridge, surrounded
by a swarm of anxious tourists,
I'd have thought I was a hopeless 1940s convict
in "the yard" on Alcatraz Island—
a mere mile and a half from the bridge.

I couldn't decide which was worse.

I looked down at my windbreaker as it
flapped uncontrollably like the flags on a frigid night
at Candlestick Park in the 1990s.

I looked at my jacket sleeve and smiled:
"WindWall Technology™"

I'm so glad they got that trademarked.

Where would we be without
WindWall Technology™ and
American ingenuity.

The Value of a College Education

Years away from a legal drink—
you have zero responsibility.

That is,
until they tell you to pick

a major

at the age of 18, sometimes 17.

They forget to tell you that the
majority of the majors offered do not
generate serious income after graduation

or ever.

They ask:
What do YOU want to DO?

You don't know yet, because you are
only 18 years old and it's not 1924.

Feeling the pressure, you settle on

uh, History—
because blood and broken promises
were always more entertaining
than algebra.

Great—sign here on the student loan application.

APPROVED!

Don't worry about it now
you don't have to pay a dime
until you graduate.

By then,
everyone will want to pay
top dollar for a History major from

Elk Ridge Valley State University!

Stop Trying So Hard

Everybody likes to label themselves,
announcing their labels aloud in work meetings:

I wear my emotions on my sleeve…
I'm very black and white
I'm OCD…
I'm a problem solver
I'm a *very* data-driven person…
I'm a positive thinker
I'm very right-brained
I tell it like it is…
I fight for what's right
I'm a very visual learner…
I'm very assertive
I'm extremely competitive…
I'm a Type A personality
I'm very left-brained
I *love* feedback
I don't sugarcoat anything
I'm at my best under pressure
I'm *very* transparent…

No, you're not.

You're a walking contradiction
like everybody else.

Now shut the fuck up!

This Man's in Charge?

There he was,
my boss.

The man who made
three times my salary,
holding my career—
at least then—
in his hands.

He poured a bowl of Lucky Charms,
then the milk,
and started eating.

What kind of grown man
eats a bowl of cereal at work?

Some fucking leader.

He talked to me
about quotas and how,
get this…

"Inputs lead to outputs."

Thanks.

He finally shoveled enough
to reach the bottom
of his bowl.

What would he do with the milk that remained?
I wondered.

He casually lifted the bowl to his mouth
and slurped.
Like a goddamn child.
This man was my boss.

How can you take
a man like that seriously?

Eat breakfast at home
or just eat
a fucking granola bar!

Working Stiffs

I did it again.
I woke wondering where it all went wrong,
what had happened,
and why the hell did I decide
to smoke cigarettes on top of it all?

A damn fool, I'll tell you.
Water.
All I want is water and a shower.
I'll brush my teeth later
I just want some water.

Sadly,
I think I'm still drunk.
Slightly.
Just enough to know it
and keep me from feeling maximum
guilt and pain.

It's either the white hat
or maybe the black,
but once I sip water
I think about champagne brunch.

Who would be willing to go with me?
Where would we go?
Is there enough time to brush,
shower, change clothes, and still
maximize an all-you-can-drink offer
with breakfast before they close?

In San Francisco,
the answer is always NO.

I can't help but yearn for the days
when this type of behavior was
expected and accepted.

They call it young,
stupid, and
"part of growing up"
when you're 23 and failing classes
at a world-renowned institution
of academic excellence
like Chico State University.

But when you're almost 40,
it's considered a "problem"
by the stiffs who are easily led.

All I can think about
is an old place in Chico
by the railroad tracks, within
walking distance from campus.

It was aptly called the Breakfast Buzz.
My god,
that is what I think about
when I think about college.

Why can't there be more places like this for adults?
Massive, greasy breakfast burritos
with NONSTOP refills of champagne.

The second you put the glass down,
a waitress who's
more hungover than you are
is there to top it off.

When the bill comes,
you only owe $27
and you can't feel your fucking legs!

The best part is,
since it's champagne,
your body,
mind,
and soul have never felt better.

You start humming the Stones and Buddy Guy's
live rendition of "Champagne and Reefer"
from Scorsese's *Shine a Light*
and your hips start shaking like Jagger's
as you make your way to
the Oasis (the O!).

It all starts making sense.

I don't even remember if it was bacon
or ham in the burrito—
who gives a shit anyway?

But those days are long gone.
Now, it's the big time,
the big city,
waitlists
and overpriced eggs
that will never touch the fucking Breakfast Buzz!

All your late-night friends
have left you for their mundane
"adult" chores
and now think of you as somebody with
a "problem" while you know damn well
they'd be at brunch with you *right now*
if it was $27 and not $138.

Fuck them,
and fuck this nonsense about
not being able to catch back-to-back buzzes.

Why should I be tied down
to the ball and chain of the establishment
just because they're too scared
to turn the fucking key they already hold?!

I'm an adult and I'll do whatever I want.
I can go by myself.
Hell, I've gone on solo road trips
to the American South,
I've been to England by myself,
I LOVE being by myself!

Drinking alone does not scare me.
I admire being alone with my own thoughts—
particularly my drunk thoughts.

I'm free to wonder,
I'm free to be critical,
I'm free to be me,
and whoever else I dream of being.

I crawl out of bed,
stretch my back,
brush my teeth,
shower,
have coffee,
and then drink Gatorade
to try and sober up.

My wife just glares at me as usual.
I consider asking her if she wants to go to brunch,
but I think better of it (Gatorade's kickin' in!),
and go water the plants
as if I hadn't been up until 5 a.m. playing guitar
and drinking whiskey
with my stupid bandana on.

I love that bandana.

I decide to stay in
and keep sipping the Gatorade.

I'm just another fucking stiff.

Say Grace

Nobody was in the kitchen
and I knew everyone's habits.
It was my moment to strike.

I entered, grabbed a granola bar,
turned around, and darted for the exit
just as I'd done successfully
every weekday morning.

Just before another
clean getaway, though,
my boss entered,

"Deno! Good morning! What's up?"

"Morning, Mark."

"Why don't I ever catch you in here
like the rest of the gang?" Mark asked.

"Because I fear small talk."

"Ha! That's great! You're a funny guy, Deno.
One thing I've always told my teams
over the years is that
'We. Are. Fa-mi-ly!'—
just like the song!

We want to build culture—

and at DataSucker, we don't leave family behind!"

I smiled, nodded, and got the hell out of there.

Four months later, DataSucker didn't get
the Series C funding they were betting on.

Mark had to give me
and eight others the bad news
on the same day.

Two months' severance.

At least I had family to lean on.

A Saturday in the Redwoods

You know you're doing good when you
sit down to take a dump
with "Ruby Tuesday"
blaring from your phone
while a space heater blows air
over the back of your left ear.

Who could hang uh name on youuuu...

Life is pretty good when you
listen to the rain tap down
from the redwoods above you
as you stare up into the skylight,
and through the trees,
as The Kinks' "Strangers"
plays in the background.

Yeah, things are going really well when you
realize you're only a quarter of the way through
the first bottle of champagne,
and the gummy is
just starting to kick in.

We are not two, we are onneeeee

Things take a turn when you
look down,
through your phone,
and at the bathroom tile

and contemplate what those before you
have done in this very bathroom,
from this very seat.

You begin to pray for a new song

(*We are not two, we are onnneeeee*).

You hit shuffle and the gods—
well above the redwoods and rain—
deliver a gift: the undeniable riff of

Chuck Berry's "Around and Around"

The gods,
they pulled strings for you.
Just you—
and *you* know it!

That riff and beat send you through the skylight
and into the stratosphere
with your pants still down like a moron!

Today is going to be a great day.

What could possibly go wrong
before the whistle blows at 10 a.m.
tomorrow morning for checkout?

Darkness in the Afternoon

Lunch is always too short.

1 p.m. meeting to discuss

nothing.

Just like most meetings.

Lunch cut short for nothing.

Everyone shifting in their chairs
holding back farts and assorted gas.
Nobody says a word, they just nod.

At what, they aren't exactly sure

Next meeting, 2:30 p.m.:

Deadlines and revenue goals
presented in eerily coded business jargon—
we learn that deadlines will be

Moved up

And revenue goals will be

Moved up

At least we learned something.

It's now 3 p.m.

Nobody does anything besides plan their next
bathroom break and wish it was 4:30 p.m.

And just like all the armies that have
never marched to anything but doom,
nobody says a word,
they just stare
in silent
compliance.

Then, suddenly,
a middle manager,
feeling the need to do
something

says,

"I love being back in the office
and collaborating again!"

Everyone just nods,
pretends to look happy,
and continues searching
for remote positions on LinkedIn.

Who is Your Master?

I'm house-sitting for a week.
The 49ers lost the Super Bowl
and I decided to drink too much Scotch.

I woke up hungover,
stepped in dog shit on my way
to the coffee maker,
and logged in
for another underpaid,
overworked Monday morning.

I went back to school
for an MBA—
because that's what FAANG
companies wanted to see.

I got into a FAANG company
because of my MBA.

I am now paid less than the market rate
for my skill set,
experience,
and education level.

The MBA clearly taught me a lot.

I received a high-performance review,
but no pay increase—

apparently, I was already "at the top"
of my level's "pay band."

I asked what would happen
if I got promoted.
They said my pay
would drop to the bottom
of the next level's pay band.

I asked to see the pay band,
but was told it was "proprietary information."

I asked if I could transfer roles
but was told I needed to be
at the next level to transfer freely.
Promotions typically take two to three years.

I don't know where I'd be without my MBA.

Corporate America #2

Circling back
Just checking in
Just following up
Does that make sense?
Right?
Let's take this offline
Apologies if this was answered already…
I was just gonna say… oh, wait, no, you go ahead…
Let's carve out some time
I'll put some time on your calendar
My calendar is up to date…
Can you see my screen?
Fireside chat
Lunch and Learn
You're on mute
Let's pull that thread…
Let's peel back the onion…
Pipeline
Prospects
Be curious…
What's your why?
What keeps you up at night?
High level
Meet them where they are…
Cascade
The back-end
Sorry, I was on mute
Unlimited vacation
Putting out fires…

I wear multiple hats
Be part of the solution, not the problem…
Thanks for taking the time…
Don't hesitate to reach out…
Great question
Headwinds
Tailwinds
Bottleneck
100%
1000%
Plus one
Work-life balance
That said…
Best
Very Best
Warmly
Best Regards
Highest Regards
Sincerely
Cheers
Respectfully
Congrats on the promotion! (bitch!)
When you get the chance…
Just to piggyback on…
We work hard and play hard
Rest and recharge
The health and safety of our employees is our *number one* priority…
Culture
Culture, Culture
Culture, Culture, Culture…
Operational efficiency
Lean environment

Economic headwinds
Unforeseen microeconomic conditions…
Streamlining operations
Headcount reduction
You're fired!

The Sound of the Rain

She was soft and warm,
with open arms

like those of a caring mother, though
there was sadness in her eyes

that had only seen the sunset
heading to and from work—

or, perhaps,
looking for work.

She just stood there now
in the embers of a slow burn,

she was a number,
not a name—

a beautiful bird
without a song.

I Wish I Could Help

It was a present without a past,
that's how I'd describe it.

There was this weight she carried,
it was back-breaking.

Enough that she smoked to remember,
but always drank to forget.

We all want to forget sometimes,
yet nothing is ever forgotten.

Sometimes, the loneliest place
is a room filled with the people
who were supposed to love you.

I Can See Clearly Now

I've seen too much in too few years—
no trust,
no honor,
no loyalty!

My hairline is receding,
my back and knees ache daily.
I am not yet forty.

Fair Pay?
Diversity, Equity, and Inclusion?
Or, "DEI," as they say…

The CEO makes 400% more than
the recent college grad
from Fartwynn State University,
$80k in debt,
for the luxury of being low-balled
for a shitty job,
for shitty pay,
and even shittier benefits.

… Oh, the American "benefits" system…

"You have to start somewhere," they tell you.
Good luck paying off those loans, Junior!

The job sucks,
but you're "lucky" to have one, they say.

Three weeks in, you realize
that Fartwynn State taught you
NOTHING about the field you're now working in.

… especially around salary negotiations…

You know more than your boss,
but nobody cares to notice,
for fear of being noticed noticing.

Eventually, you're "let go,"
not for poor performance,
but because the company
couldn't balance the books—
now you are the one who must suffer.

Now unemployed,
behind on student loan payments,
you read that the CEO–who oversaw the hiring
of the CFO–
received a $300k *bonus*,
for doing all the firings and then
graciously "stepping down."

You hit the job boards,
connect with a couple of recruiters via LinkedIn
and job applications and interviews commence.

One recruiter tells you
your resume "*has* to be one page."

The other, of course,
says that it doesn't matter

and that "*all* of your experience
and volunteer work should be highlighted"—
regardless of the number of pages.

One tells you that you need to
leverage your "alumni network,"
the other politely tells you
nobody cares about Fartwynn State University.

You go to the alumni webpage
for Fartwynn State
only to be directed to
a "page under construction" notice.

You apply to hundreds of jobs
and sit through dozens of
sales interviews with too many rounds.

No luck.

You scratch your head and wonder how
any modern and self-respecting company
still requires a cover letter.

"Well, how will they know you *really* want the job?"
one recruiter asks you.

"Because I just fucking applied!"
you impatiently respond.

… Disgruntled, and wishing your parents were rich
so you wouldn't have to deal with all this nonsense…

You sip a **PBR** on your futon because
all nine micro-breweries in the area
are now too expensive.

Plus, you realize that at some point,
all the "Skull-Fucker Double **IPAs**"
end up tasting the same anyway,
and eventually, eight of those breweries will go under
and all of their employees who bought into the dream
will be on their respective futons drinking fucking **PBR**
just like you!

Ah, sip it in, pal—it's Corporate America, baby!
You've seen all you need to see
and it's only been one goddamn year.

Just Enough Salt in the Stew

Deep in thought
well beyond the horizon,
it's a constant push and pull

The necktie stranglehold
gets tighter
and tighter

Soap bubbles dance in the distance,
their rainbow skins shine like the quarterly
quota accelerators—

close enough to pop,
but the pesky wind blows them just
out of reach

And the handcuffs—
they shine like pure gold,
but feel like nickel-plated steel

It's like biting into a vinegar potato chip,
and thinking *this* will be the time
you actually like them

The Entrepreneur

(A man with full-sleeve tattoos and hair just long enough to be nearing the threshold for a hairnet requirement is found dead, hanging in his Chinatown apartment, by his girlfriend of seven years.)

Approximately 127 minutes prior…

"Well," he said, squirming uncomfortably in his chair.

"I make everything fresh daily, and we only use the freshest, most seasonal ingredients. It's a farm-to-table operation."

Silence.

"Mm-hmm," said the junior loan officer at ABC Community Bank.

"I mean, my biggest influence is my grandmother. Her dishes have always inspired me and I infuse each of my dishes with that passion."

The loan officer's desk light now seemed to emit more heat than the heat lamps that burned through the aspiring chef's expo line.

"Right. Okay, yeah, so we won't be moving forward with your restaurant loan application."

West Marin, In Us All

The cicadas sang their song,
although I feel like they're always out of tune
and still get away with it.
Nobody to answer to, I suppose.

I finally went to Spirit Rock,
but they were closed for a private retreat.

I'd been trying to go there for years now
but it never quite worked out right.
I planned everything perfectly today
but that was a minor hiccup.

I hope those techie pricks enjoy their retreat
miming, "Hare Krishna"
in their stupid Patagonia vests!

I'm back at my cabin in the redwoods
and I wish it actually was mine.

There's nothing like being so close
to everything you need,
but feeling so far away.
Sometimes, at least.

I drove from Fairfax
to the Point Reyes Lighthouse—
an hour and ten minutes' drive.
What a drive.

The cool morning air drifting
through lush green hills
filled with grazing cows
who haven't a care in the world.

I could be stuck in a boring work meeting
where middle managers continue
sending nothing to my mind!
Or hearing a client complain about something
I simply cannot fix.

But instead,
I'm driving—virtually all alone
on Sir Francis Drake Blvd
and nearing the lighthouse.

What views!
The hillsides,
the Pacific Ocean,
the deer, the cows, the coyote!

I pulled over and took pictures along the road
because there was **NOBODY** else around
and god, what a feeling that was.

The lighthouse stood proud—
historic and carefully preserved,
it marked the furthest west in Marin
I'd ever been.

I'll be back,
and I just want to share those views
and beautiful peace with everyone I can.

Not only friends and family,
but all my corporate enemies too!

What I felt and witnessed today in West Marin—
well, it could end all wars,
and I'm confident of that.

Now it's a hot shower,
a strong gummy,
pizza,
some good red—
and that guitar over in the corner that's
just giving me the fucking eye.

Rain is coming,
but it can't bring me down—
not today, baby.

Happy Hour

It's still dark at 11 a.m.;
no, it's not the fog.

It's consuming,
like a close talker.

No break is imminent,
and I'm getting antsy.

They say,
 "You don't get a rainbow until you get the rain."

Rage

Rage, not like the classic college kegger
Rage, not like the type where a dopey kid
talks about something popular

But,

Rage, like when you realize it's last call
Rage, when you realize your last credit's up on the
jukebox
Rage, when the bill comes at a sub-par restaurant in
San Francisco
Rage, when you update your iPhone and it
automatically slows down

Or,

Rage, when you realize most people are idiots
Rage, when you realize those idiots have votes
Rage, when uneducated morons get angry when
predatory college loans are forgiven

And finally,

RAGE, when you realize who your wife's new
"friend" really is
RAGE, when "Dear Doctor" by the Rolling Stones
won't cure the pain anymore
RAGE, when you realize all you have left is a bottle
of well whiskey
RAGE, when the alarm goes off on Monday
morning

Slide Through Your Hands

What does one do after a divorce?

I can't imagine having to get used to the scent
of another woman.

Everyone has a scent;
it's on their clothes,
in their house,
and their parents and siblings have
virtually the same scent.

What if it's musky,
do you just get used to it?

What if *I'm* musky,
does she just have to get used to it?

Out of all the guys I can be,
which one will I pull out for our first date?

How much do I reveal?
How will I feel when she doesn't text back?

And then there's the morning breath…
everyone has it.
Some worse than others,
but we ALL have it.

Is she a snorer?
Teeth grinder?
Rude to waitstaff?

I can't take it!

The term itself sounds like it was created
just to ruin your day:

"*D-I-V-O-R-C-E*"

Everyone thinks something is wrong with you…
What did *you* do?

Do you write her family a letter?
Handwritten or typed?

Do you move out of the city?
Why should I?
It's just as much mine as hers,
theirs, and anyone else's!

But I know I'll run into every one of them
while in North Beach.
I know it.

Do we hug?
Will they stiffen up if we hug?
Or will they just pretend not to notice me?
Would I pretend not to notice them?

Probably.

Everybody wants a smoking gun:

"What happened, was *he* cheating?"
"What happened, did *he* get physical?"
"What happened, did *she* have enough
of the late-night music sessions?"
"What happened, did *he* get sick
of the emotional instability?"
"What happened, did *she* punch *him*
in the face for the third time?"

Sometimes good people just drift apart
and what once was seamless conversation
now becomes friction to the point of loneliness.

Love is cruel,
love is elusive,
and love is extremely
hard to find.

But sometimes we can feel it,
we can taste it,
and we can live it…
until it vanishes like a dream.

Good-Time Deno

Good-Time Deno comes 'round
Saturday nights

Good-Time Deno always singin'
the news!

I'm a hell of a salesman,
do you know how I know that?

I can get anyone to have another round
I can overcome any objection
I can get you to stay later
I can get you laughing
I can get you to realize

even for a short time,

that I'm a major asset to you.

I can get you to go against
your own best judgment.

I just wish my bosses understood that.

Good-Time Deno comes 'round
Monday morning,

Good-Time Deno always singin'
the blues!

Lines

And there they were
two lines down my face
just to the side of my mouth, under my nose
all the way down to my lip.

Lines

I wasn't even hungover either
It was just another boring,
sober, Wednesday night
waiting for the alarm to go off
to work for the Man on Thursday.

Lines

I stared at the greys in my beard
and then down at the tube of
"Anti-Aging" cream…

I contemplated throwing it away.
I looked up at my forehead.

Lines

I put the cream on:
a *generous* portion, just as recommended.

Slide Through My Hands

You finally realize it's over
when the place is empty.

Nothing left but echoes of
crying,
stomping feet on hardwood
and the eerie sound of silence
after yet another big fight.

It's like death,
but worse.

You're both still
living and breathing—
probably more freely now—
but you're there alright.

Her scent lingers in the
nearly empty apartment
as you think of those
who came before you and
all who'll surely come after.

Were they as miserable?
Or were their days filled with
joy, laughter and passionate sex?

Then you remember the good—
the vibrant times when things were
made with love rather than spite.

The small things that mattered:
surprise turkey sandwiches for lunch,
handwritten notes welcoming you home
from a long trip,
and surely,
the inaugural application
of "Just For Men."

The tears finally come—
a soft patter on the hardwood
of the soulless bedroom
that once had
hope.

They keep falling,
like February rain—
washing away the pain of one,
only to hand the keys
to some unknown other.

They can't say we never tried.

Harmony

It doesn't exist in marriage
nor in school

It doesn't exist at work
nor with family

It only exists in nature
or sometimes at a solid dive bar

Harmony is payday
it is truth

Harmony is the Everly Brothers
not Twitter

The Search Continues

Maybe the one I need is too far away,
out of touch, and out of time.

Maybe she lives in rural Arkansas?
Or what about Nebraska?
No, nothing good ever comes out of those states!

Maybe she works at Applebee's?
Chevys?
No, no, it would be a Michelin-starred place
if she worked in food service!

How about a Chief People Officer?
Whatever it is they do.
Maybe she's a seamstress?
No, no, no, she'd be modeling the dress,
not making it, goddamnit!

Maybe it's not her who's missing after all.

Illumination

Illumination can be painfully bright.

Especially when it shines from above.
You know you don't have a chance,
for the light is always right.

What are you hiding, boy?
North Beach stars
are hidden by fog.

Can't ya' sing?
We see you preen—
now come spin like a goddamn toy!

The morning light comes,
you don't like what you see,
nowhere to run now, boy,
it's just you and me.

It's blinding,
and you're down to
your last strike,
now just remember,

illumination can be painfully bright.

Don't Let Me Down

When my father was sick,
I drove him to the doctor
in my brown Chevy Blazer.

He bought it for me on my 18th birthday,
reluctantly, because (as only he could put it),
"Deno, it's shit-brown!
Why the hell would you want
to be seen driving that thing?"

I can't imagine my answer,
but he bought the damn car,
and I remember him saying

—like all men of that age—

"I got a great deal!
You should've seen me work that guy.
I still got it, baby!"

Four years later,
we were driving down Park Ave in Chico,
past the lot where he bought the car.

On the CD player,
The Beatles' *Let It Be* played,
and "Don't Let Me Down" came on—
Phil Spector's version,
with his Wall of Sound.

It wasn't by design,
just the CD I had in.
I was taking him to chemo,
where that brutal assault of
"treatment"

would undoubtedly let him down.

Neither of us said a word
as John Lennon belted
the gut-wrenching chorus—
I just kept driving.

We could both feel the tension
and through the side mirror,
I could see his eyes welling up.

Maybe a flash of youth—
him beating away
on his '64 blue-sparkle Ludwig kit
for all the beautiful girls
on a hot Chico summer day in 1969.

Or maybe he felt
he was letting *me* down,
knowing he wouldn't be there
to answer all the questions
he said I'd have for him
as I got older.

He was right about all those questions,
but he never let me down.
Never.

And as I sign the papers
for a brand-new SUV,
I smile, thinking of him—
and figure he'd be proud,
not for the purchase itself,
but because
I chose the color green.

RIP Soul

I am a human
I am writing this,
right now.

I hate my job
I'm lucky to have a job
you know, insurance and all.

I am a human
I am writing this,
right now.

I have a soul
Corporate America is
sucking it out of me.

I am a human
I am writing this,
right now,

while enduring a training
about something that will
eventually replace me.

It was paid for by the company.

I am a human
I am...

Wildhoney

I imagine it in the rolling green hills of West Marin—
Nicasio, Olema, or maybe Bolinas?

Yeah, it's Bolinas.

I imagine it just past Smiley's Saloon and Bo Gas,
a left turn onto Mesa Road.

Oh, wildhoney.

Past the fire station,
I smell it, it's within reach.

Life ain't bad, baby.

Left on Overlook Drive
slow down to twenty-five—*just* enough to feel the
cool ocean breeze through the window.

The wildhoney draws nearer.

Right turn on Elm,
finally, a right.

It's between here and the Pacific.

Out of the car and walking towards it,
I know the way now.

I lift the gate and wander into Sally's garden
where I know the wildhoney awaits.

Soft gravel underfoot, each step careful,
so as not to disturb the delicate wildlife.

Each step seems to make the chirp of the birds
ring clearer,

the emerging sunshine
brighter,

and the koi pond
more tranquil.

Colors everywhere.

Surrounded by succulents,
native and rare plants—
a life lived and a future ahead.

This is a place
where even the trees' dreams come true.

I can barely see Sally on the deck,
her face still swallowed by the low morning fog,
as watercolors masquerade across her canvas.

The color and inspiration outpace the fog,
felt with any sense you choose.
To have all at once is the king's lot,
a true privilege many take for granted.

I can rest now.

At peace with my wildhoney,
koi pond, and the Pacific Ocean—
the sound of its distant waves
dissolving the pain inside me.

Somewhere Else

Will it ever be worth anything—
the time we put into a "career"?

Will it ever make me proud—
the things I do for a "living"?

Would I be happier at Green Apple—
just punching in and moving the stacks?

Would I smile more often—
just pointing people in the right direction?

Maybe I'll retire to Greece—
maybe I'll pack it all in…

(Here come the corny lines…)

In Greece, I won't count the money,
I'll just sip tea with Ikaria honey.

In Greece, I'll sleep till noon.
In America, it's all doom and gloom.

Preventative Health

I take fourteen supplement pills per day,
carefully divided across seven different brands
for an average of two pills per bottle, per brand.

The pills range from general health to
gut health
and stress balancing.

These are very expensive,
not covered by insurance,
and **HIGHLY** recommended by my doctor.

I exercise daily,
and do yoga—
sometimes morning and night.

Average six to eight hours of sleep per night,
light tai chi three to four days a week,
meditate and practice gratitude daily.

I eat fast food only once a year,
regularly see a shrink,
and have enlightening hobbies.

I get my blood tested annually,
a physical exam too—
I beg the doctors to test

for more

than just basic panels (a request that they always deny!)
I even drink green tea once a day.

But I still get fucking sick
twice a year like everyone else!

Chairman of the Broads

He was a Little League All-Star
batted a thousand

He was a Pop Warner icon
led all of L.A. in interceptions

He opened doors I thought were closed

He worked out seven days a week
never missed a leg day

He fucked all the waitresses
made more tips than all

He called himself "Dr. Ha Ha"

He introduced me to La Rocca's
and my buddy Lee

He introduced me to Brautigan
and the three-day bender

He was always a step ahead

He stuck it to the line cooks,
the head chef,
the GM,
and the goddamn owner of the restaurant!

But when the lights came on,
he was just a drunken,
regular ol' schnook.

Something I Already Had

You told me to go find something
that I already had.

And as I sit by this dirty river,
I watch our love
float on by.

Yes, it floats on by.

Dreams gain shape,
and then they dissolve,
this life we live—

It just floats on by.

They told me to find something
that I already had.

But as I watch this dirty river,
I feel my being
float on by.

It just floats on by.

You know this ain't my
first time around—
Lord never hears my pleas.

As I watch this dirty river,
I know it will never reach the sea.

Going Down Slow

I used to work at a startup.
I had a colleague I liked there and
he could sense the impending doom
just as well as I could.

Naturally, he and I spent most of our days
commiserating.

We'd find time to head out
and take long walks to bullshit and kill time,
anything to get out of that terrible open office.

(By the way, whoever thought of the open office
concept should publicly have their ass kicked and the
video shared on TikTok.)

We'd always laugh as we waited for the elevator
to take us from the office to the lobby

and freedom beyond.

As we waited,
hoping we wouldn't have to awkwardly
share it with other colleagues,
we'd crack up as the automated voice
announced,

GOING DOWN.

We'd giggle like kids and say it was a euphemism
for our careers at the cash-strapped company,
especially as we watched the premium snacks
and coffee turn generic,
and the cringeworthy happy hours
nobody wanted to be at
go from once a week to once a month.

One day—
just our goddamn luck—
the company COO came to the elevator
as we were about to board.

"Hi Ken," we both said like pussies who knew
they'd be fired in six months' time.

"Gentlemen," he nodded back
clearly not knowing either of our names.

But, unexpectedly,
Ken asked,

"Geno and Alex, right?"

"Close—but Deno and Andrew, actually, sir,"

I sheepishly replied.

"*GOINNNNGGG DOWWWNNNN,*"
the elevator declared.

Andrew and I squirmed,
trying to hold back laughter.

"Of course. Apologies, guys."

Seven excruciating seconds passed until
the elevator door finally opened.

Ken cleared his throat,
adjusted his blazer lapels, and exited first.

We followed a step behind,
but as all three of us already knew,
the walk from the elevator to the building door
was long and there was no way you could
make that walk without the need to strike up

MORE

AWKWARD

CONVERSATION!

Realizing this, Ken peeled off
and faked an abrupt phone call.

"Sorry guys, I gotta take this,"
he said as he waved us on toward freedom.

A moment before,
I'd thought about doing the same.
I did, I swear,
but he beat me to it.

An executive decision indeed.
Swift and confident.

Maybe that's why he got paid the big bucks
and my buddy and I were underpaid, overqualified
and on our way to fucking Subway!

Once we were safely outside,
Andrew, pretending to be Ken,
joked,

"Hey Siri,

Remind me to fire Gino and Adam
when I get back to the office."

We laughed hysterically
and I suggested we make it a drinking lunch.

Nobody knew we were gone anyway.

La Rocca's, Off the Clock

Cousin Joe used to hang out there too.

One of his favorite spots,
right across from his own playground.

I got a blowjob in the bathroom
there once (actually, a couple of times).

Did a bunch of blow in there too
(more than a couple of times).

I blew up that bathroom
(many times).

I've been punched
in the face there (only once).

Listened to "Beast of Burden"
and "Werewolves of London"
on the old jukebox
on repeat
many a late night
(*Ah-hoooo, werewolves of London/Ah-hooo*).

Sat alone on Thanksgiving there.
Wrote a song in there.

Watched my bus pass by there,
many a night.

Watched a friend bomb
at an open mic night.

Cousin Joe sat in the corner,
sipped his beer and read the paper.

Didn't want to be bothered.
He was real old-fashioned.

This is why the blowjob,
the coke,
and the diarrhea
all took place in the bathroom
under the photo of Babe Ruth.

Lightness & Darkness

Weed,   Wine,   Music,
Gummy,   Red,   Zeppelin,
High,   Thackrey,   Tangerine,

Work,   Coffee,   Elevator,
Meetings,   Black,   Small talk

Kill. Me. Now.

Competing Demands

There I was,
getting my picture taken
in front of the Ben Franklin statue in
Washington Square Park.

Just like Brautigan.

It was my second cover shoot
for *Rolling Stone* magazine;
only this time,
the crowds following us
around North Beach
were even bigger.

"One more against the statue,"

—demanded Annie Leibovitz, as she snapped away
at me.

"Alright, that's enough.
We gotta get him outta here before this mob of
college girls tears him to pieces
and he has to break their little hearts,"
—demanded my bodyguard, Big Ed.

Away we went into the waiting black limousine
while the girls pounded at the tinted glass,
demanding just a glimpse.

"Hawaii West,"—I ordered my driver.

"Great choice, the lighting will be great in there,"
—Annie confirmed,
never actually having been there.

"Excellent choice, sir,"—the driver confirmed
as he drove the two short blocks towards Vallejo
and Powell.

"I like it, boss.
Will be hard for 'um to track us down there.
Make sure to park in the damn garage!"—Big Ed
confirmed my choice
and demanded of the driver, in an attempt to avoid
the screaming girls.

As usual,
when we arrived at the bar,
nobody was around.

Just the way I preferred it.

I lit up a smoke as Sunny,
the bartender, emerged from the darkness,
poured drinks, and demanded payment immediately.

Nearby, a couch sat tucked behind the bar stools—
its leather worn from years of stories
told by men forgotten before they were remembered.

I took a hit of my Camel
while Annie snapped away
and Big Ed paid the tab.

"I've shot Dylan,

Lennon,

McCartney,

and *Jagger*,

But *YOU* have the *IT* factor, Deno,"
—Annie shouted over camera clicks
and Sunny angrily bitching aloud
about her 80% tip.

Almost on cue,
three gorgeous ladies
stopped dead in their tracks
outside the door.

"Oh my god. It's him!"
—one squealed as she pounded on the door,
demanding somebody let her in.

Big Ed knew the drill.
He ran over to the door,
cracked it, and looked around to make
sure there wouldn't be a stampede.

Then, after checking IDs,
he let them in.

"It's really him.
Fuck, that's him!"—the one said again
while covering her mouth in shock.

"Are you *really hiiim?*"
—the second friend excitedly asked.

The third just stared.
Almost trance-like,
deep into my eyes.

She knew it was me.

"Annie, Eddie,"—I commanded,
taking another drag from my Camel.

"Let's hold on the pictures for a bit.
Time to give these beautiful ladies a glimmer,"
—I said through a cloud of smoke.

"Sir, we have dinner in two hours with the mayor
and his wife,"
—Big Ed reminded me,

"Cancel it,"—I instructed him.

Without as much as a head nod,
Big Ed called for a round of drinks for my new friends
and paid Sunny enough for multiple rounds and
whisked Annie away to the car
and back to the Fairmont Hotel where we'd all
reconvene for more pictures later.

Sometimes the constant flash
and clicking of the camera
was too much to take.

Even for a celebrity like me.

Finally alone with the girls on the couch,
I mesmerized them with my tales of the road:
selling out multiple nights at the Garden,
my vast musical insights,
and of course,
stories of how my masterpieces came to fruition.

Sunny grumbled,
turned her back to the action
and zoned out to her Korean soap operas
while Van Morrison's "Glad Tidings"
hummed from the jukebox speakers overhead.

As the tension built,
the third girl couldn't take it anymore
and her deep gaze turned to a passionate kiss
as she grabbed the back of my head,
forcing my lips to hers.

The two others unbuckled my belt—
one, giggling with excitement,
demanded,
"Guess which one of us it *isss*,"
as they both ducked their heads.

I tilted my head back
and just as I was about to play the
"Guess Who" game,

I woke up,

alone in my Chinatown apartment,
with an hour to spare
before needing to be at the office
to sell print advertising
to people who only wanted digital.

Have Backbone, Disagree and Commit

It's the feeling you get
when you finally learn
the guitar riff to your
favorite song.

You now know
that you can carry it with you
and play it whenever you want.

Not just in your head anymore.

It's the feeling you get
when the Man demands you
return to the office—

after you made the company ten million
on a six-million-dollar goal
while working from home.

It's the feeling you get
when some corporate lackey,
balls-deep in the punchbowl,
says with a straight face:

"Why don't you get a side hustle,
make some extra money?"
instead of fighting for
what you've both rightfully earned.

And you think:

"Isn't that what this full-time
job is for, you fucking asshole?!"

It's the feeling you get
when HR assumes you aren't
taking screenshots of EVERYTHING
and forwarding to your personal email.

It's the feeling you get
when you finally quit
and they ask:
"How can we get better?"

It's the feeling you get
when you sit down for lunch

at the bar

inside North Beach Restaurant
and order a gin martini
with blue cheese olives
on a Monday.

It Never Gets Old

City skyline shines brightly—
the neon lights of Broadway more enticing
than the Vegas Strip.

Opportunity awaits,
I can't lose.

And yet I don't mind being stuck
in bridge traffic,
not at all.

The city skyscrapers glow.
The grunts return Monday
to deliver their busy work—
on time and under budget.

For now, the silent concrete
shivers in the night cold—
lonely with anticipation.

The Golden Gate in the distance
lights up with hope,
like a pulse in the night
reaching for a better future.

The Alcatraz lighthouse blinks on—
a timed reminder to make
wise decisions
in North Beach tonight.

I have it all mapped out:

Gino & Carlo,
Specs',
Vesuvio
and finally,

Hawaii West.

Goddamn, it's good to be back
home,

to everyone else's
vacation.

North Beach Wailin' Blues

For Willie Nelson
North Beach, 2016

They got the honky tonks in Nashville,
and the outlaw singin' in Texas,
but nobody's got, and I mean nobody's got
the North Beach Wailin' Blues.

I'm livin' yesterday's tomorrow
filled with tears of constant sorrow.
But when I'm down
I keep searchin' 'round
for that North Beach Wailin' Blues.

I got empty pockets,
a burned-up nose,
yeah, I'm broke
in mind, body, and soul.

Thought everyone's my friend,
bought another round again,
still in search of that North Beach Wailin' Blues.

I got whiskey bottles,
a bloodied nose,
and a beat-up pair of shoes.

It's closin' time again,
better make it one more gin,

keep singing' that North Beach Wailin' Blues.

I'm livin' yesterday's tomorrow,
filled with tears of constant sorrow,
but when I'm down,
I keep searchin' 'round
for that North Beach Wailin' Blues.

Yeah, my pickup truck got towed today,
yet another casualty on street cleanin' day.

My pockets feel empty,
down to my last buck,
better head to North Beach and
turn 'round my luck!

I drop ten in the slot,
it's two on the dot,
time for those Rollin' Stones *agaaaiinn*

Work can wait,
She's got hips that shake
honey, don't you make me choose.

Cause when I'm down
I keep searching 'round
for that North Beach Wailin' Blues.

Moonlight Mile

A warm Sunday and Monday in North Beach, 2021.

A great time is ahead.

Bloody Marys at the Showdown,
slices of Tony's Pizza,
Peronis, and mid-shelf white wine
with friends in Washington Square Park.

Sunshine and beautiful vibes all around—
North Beach days

Friends start to disperse, first in pairs,
then one by one.
They have work tomorrow.

I push forward,
testing the limits of my body,
mind,
and other people's patience.

Drinks at Tupelo,
Gino & Carlo,
down to Vesuvio,
and on to Grasslands.

No dinner—
North Beach nights

Then
I make my way to Hawaii West.

Busier than usual this close to closing time.

A guy has the jukebox;
he looks like he's from Modesto or somewhere similar.
He plays something incomprehensible.
Just riff-bashing mayhem with no discernible lyrics.

Trash.

I wait until his last song to make my move.
That's class.
I take control and slip in my cash.

Pressure's on though—
I can feel it in the way he glares at me
and smacks his disgusting lips,
like only someone from Modesto can do.

I think to myself:

Nobody comes to MY bar
in MY city
and tells ME how to play MY Jukebox!

I play eight straight Stones songs, just to prove a point:

1. "It's Only Rock 'n Roll (But I Like It)" (Live,
   Love You Live, 1977)
2. "Jumpin' Jack Flash" (Live, '*Get Yer Ya-Ya's Out!*'
   1970)

3. "Start Me Up" (Live, *Hyde Park Live*, 2013)
4. "All Down the Line" (Live, *Some Girls: Live in Texas '78*, 2011)
5. "Honky Tonk Women" (Studio Single, 1969)
6. "Crazy Mama" (*Black and Blue*, 1976)
7. "Rocks Off" (*Exile on Main St.*, 1972)
8. "Shattered" (Live, *Some Girls: Live in Texas '78*, 2011)

I dance,
I sing,
and do the best damn Jagger impression around.

I am him.
For just a fleeting moment in time,
I am really *him*.

I am not a corporate 'earn-ie',
not tonight,
not on MY TIME,
I am who I want to be
in this very moment.

I'm drenched in sweat,
and the people—my fans?—all wonder,
"How the fuck has he not tripped yet?
He's tanked!"

But I don't,
because when you're being yourself,
it comes naturally.

'Guns,' however, has heard and seen enough.

They don't move like that in Modesto,
and he steps back to the jukebox for another run.

He plays:

1. Something by Puddle of Mudd
2. Something by Godsmack

Only two songs? He must be out of cash.

I sip my gin and make my way to the jukebox
to end this amateur's night
and send him back to Modesto in a body bag.

"No more Rolling Stones songs, bud,"
he says with a shit-threat-grin,
casually lining up his pool shot.

"I'm not in the fuckin' mood, pal.
Now shut the fuck up,"
I snap back with the confidence of a man
who knows his opponent
gets nervous in big city traffic.

We step toward each other,
and his 6'2" frame
towers over me at 5'8."

"We got a big guy here!" he jokes to his hideous friend,
another mouth-breathing inbred from out of town,
as he looks down at me.

"Yeah, sure thing, man.

I don't want any problems.
Sometimes I get excited and try to
talk my way into
a higher weight class,"
I admit, trying to calm the scene.

"Sure thing, *Hoss*,"
he fires back, sounding like a dipshit hick.

Now, 'bud' was one thing,
but 'big guy' and 'Hoss'?
Well, I needed to retaliate.

Without hesitation
I turn around and play:

"Get Off Of My Cloud" by the Stones,
while simultaneously letting out a blood-curdling,
"Woo! Let's go, baby!"

And before the guitar riff can
come in behind the iconic drum intro,
we're already engaged in battle.

He throws me against the wall,
and my head hits the side of the jukebox.
I'm *alive* again—
just in time to catch a flurry
of punches from this animal.

Attempting to get out of his farmhand's grip,
I let loose my vaunted left hook,
but after drinking since noon,

it comes out as more of a right elbow
that never lands.
It's not going well for me.

It's normal barfight commotion;
Bartender Sunny, in her thick accent, wails,
"Knock it off, ass-uh-holes!"

A chair goes down,
and a scream or two comes from the one
female patron in attendance,
until finally,
the owner, Nolan,
comes out to save my ass.

As the real Mick sings on,
(It's three a.m., there's too much noise,
don't you people ever wanna go to beeeddd?)

Nolan grabs Big Country by the neck
and throws him off me with ease.

"Get the fuck out of here!
Both of you, goddamnit! NOW!"
he yells at the two outsiders,
while throwing their jackets at their cowboy boots.

"Deno, get your ass over there,"
Nolan screams as he points at the wall
opposite the jukebox.

"But I got more credits, baby,"
I drunkenly plead,

blood dripping down the side of my head.

"Now!"
he orders,
like he's talking to a 4-year-old.

The few stragglers at the bar close up
and shuffle off without a word. It's past 2 a.m.

Nolan keeps a close eye outside,
then locks up for the night
and unplugs the jukebox.

I'm the only paying customer left.

Nolan talks for a bit,
laughing at me
for trying to take on the big fella.

He lays back in his leather jacket
on the couch behind my bar chair
and starts snoring like a man
who's just spent six days on the road.

Another man down—
North Beach mornings.

I smile sweetly,
knowing later today,
when he turns on the jukebox,
he'll be promptly reminded of me

—when he's greeted by seven more Stones songs—

just what a man needs when hungover.

Sunny wipes the bartop with a dirty towel,
muttering her usual insults in Korean.

She pours me a gin and herself a tequila,
no doubt adding them both to my tab.

I ask Sunny if I can play
one
more
song.

She agrees,
and finally speaks to me:
"But no more Rolling Stones, ass-uh-hole!"

I grab my phone and play

"Moonlight Mile" by the Rolling Stones.

As Nolan's snoring gets drowned out
by the grand instrumentation
and hauntingly beautiful melody
of the song spilling softly from my phone on the
worn bartop,
we both smoke our cigarettes
and look in opposite directions.

For what, we're not sure.

Nobody says a word.

I stare at the smoke slowly rising
deep into the dimly hung lights
as the final refrain of the song lands—
cymbals crashing and Mick's voice bellowing,
through the darkness, into the light of hope.

Past the smoke,
my eyes barely focus on the wall clock.
It always reminds me
of the clock in every classroom
from elementary through high school.

It's exactly 2:49 a.m.

I have to work in 6 hours and 11 minutes.
I'm not worried,
because the best part about working from home
is that they can't smell your breath.

And of course, 11 minutes is plenty of time
to stumble up to Powell and Washington St.
to hear the humming of the cable car
tracks, precisely at 3 a.m.

Who knows, maybe I'll even get a free nightcap.

About the Author

Deno Gell is a poet and the founder of *Gell Studio Presents*, a platform for poetry and lyrical expression. His debut collection, *Dreaming of North Beach (from Corporate America)*, draws from years spent straddling two worlds: the corporate halls of the tech industry and the dive bars, backstreets, and poetic after-hours of San Francisco. Shaped by music, burnout, and the city itself, his voice explores the absurdity, ache, and dark humor of modern life.

Originally from Chico, California, Deno has lived and worked in San Francisco since 2010.

Follow him on Instagram: @thegellstudio